Tell the world!

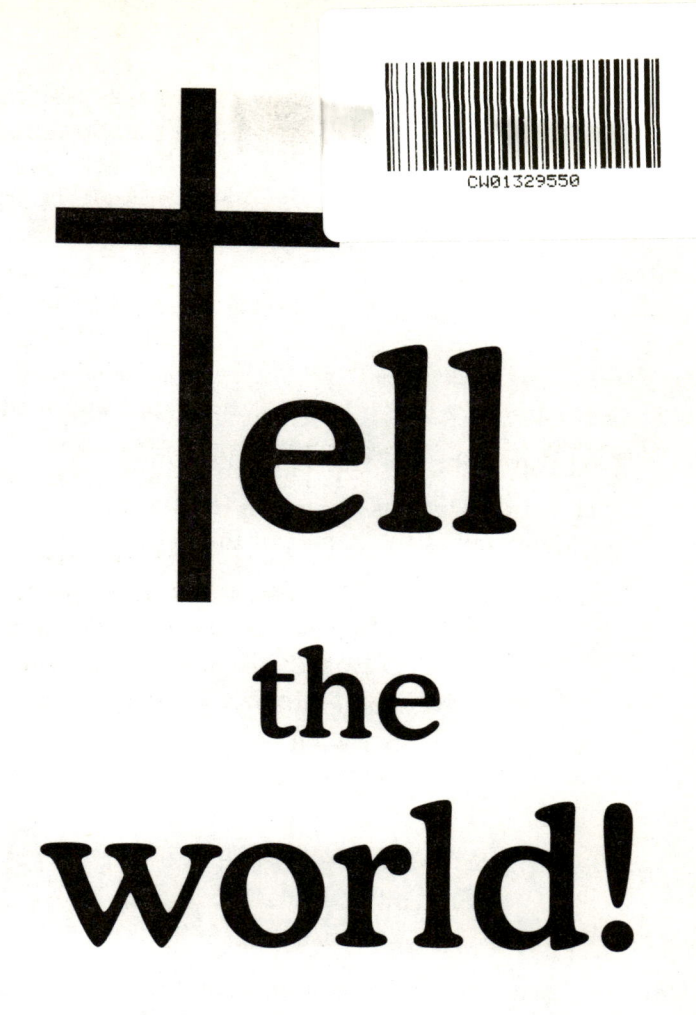

True stories that reveal the faithfulness of the living God

Terry-Anne Preston

with foreword by Fiona Castle

Text copyright © Terry-Anne Preston 2002

The author asserts the moral right to be identified as the author of this work.

Published by
The Framework Trust
P O Box 293
Newton Flotman
Norwich
NR15 1TW

ISBN: 0-9543044-0-3
First published 2002

All rights reserved

Unless otherwise stated Scripture quotations are taken from the King James Version of the Bible.

Foreword

For many people, the mere thought of having to share our faith causes us to freeze with fear, and to speak in public – out of the question! Yet, in a very gentle way, Terry-Anne helps us to realize that it is possible.

I have found Terry-Anne's book, "Tell the World," challenging and encouraging from start to finish. Her anecdotes of how she learned to listen to God and then put into practice what she felt Him saying, a very powerful lesson for us all.

I share Terry-Anne's heart, to tell the world, because as Christians, Jesus calls us to make disciples, and Paul said, "I am made all things to all men, that I might by all means save some." (1Cor 9:22)

This book gives us the "how to" appropriately and without embarrassment and with action plans and goals. I hope it will be widely read, because I am sure it will be a very valuable asset.

Fiona Castle

Acknowledgements

Have you heard the story of the mouse trap?

A farmer was concerned about the growing mouse problem on his farm and so he decided to buy some traps. A mouse looked through the hole in the wall and saw him prepare the traps. "Oh no!" he exclaimed and he ran around the farm telling the other animals about it. The chicken wasn't worried. "I can see this is of concern to you," he clucked, "but it really has nothing to do with me."

The mouse went to the pig and told him about the traps. "I am so very sorry for you," said the pig, "I will pray for you but it is really of no concern to me." The mouse went home, feeling very alone.

That night a sound could be heard in the farmhouse. The farmer's wife rushed to see if the mouse had been caught in the trap. In the darkness, she failed to see that the trap had caught the tail of a snake and the snake turned and bit the famer's wife. The farmer rushed her to hospital and she eventually was allowed home but with a fever.

In order to make her feel better, the farmer decided to make her fresh chicken soup. He took his axe and delivered a fatal blow to the chicken. The soup was delicious but the farmer's wife got worse and eventually died.

Her family and friends came to the funeral and in order to feed them, the farmer took the axe one more time and dealt a fatal blow to the pig. The pork was delicious.

The moral of the story? When you hear of someone near you who is having difficulty, remember that when there is a rat trap in the house, the whole farmyard is at risk.

When they heard that I planned to write this book, a number of people, unlike the chicken or pig, did not turn away and leave me to it. They decided, instead, to get involved and help. For that kindness, I am extremely grateful.

Becky Taylor, Lisa Gregory and Dawn Davidson offered to help in a very special way by being guinea pigs to test out the action plan at the end of this book. They have freely offered to share their own stories of faith and I warmly encourage you to read them.

Di Latham and Rick Golko applied their eagle eyes to the manuscript and layout and helpfully pointed out a number of errors in the initial drafts. If any mistakes have remained in this final version, the responsibility for that is entirely mine and not theirs!

Many thanks, too, to Fiona Castle, who was so willing to offer a foreword and words of encouragement.

The Framework Trust Prayer Pool have prayed around the world for the formation and distribution of this book. If you are impacted by it in any way, it is likely to be as a result of their prayers.

Finally, but maybe most importantly, I acknowledge the help and inspiration of God – my father. Without his amazing work over the last twenty years, the stories outlined in the following pages would not be here to tell.

My desire and heartfelt prayer, is that you will discover as you read, just how much God loves you and desires that you share that love with others. He loves you so much, He wants you to shout it from the rooftops; to sing it from the choir stalls; in short, to tell the world!

Terry-Anne Preston

Contents

Foreword. 3
Acknowledgements 5
Introduction 9
62 Piles of Grass 13
The Art of Prayer. 19
Top of the Pops. 21
House of Prayer 25
    Moneyless Mortgage 25
    One Hour or Less 27
    Choral Conifers 30
Does God Contradict Himself?. 33
    Around the World 33
    13 Years Later 35
It's a Dog's Life! 39
    Right There Where He Always Was 40
Wiped Out 47
Plane Prayers 51

How to Tell The World

How to Tell the World 57
Why Tell Our Story? 59
Are All Stories to be Made Public? 61
Who Could Benefit from My Story? 63
Medium for Communicating the Story. 67
Techniques Jesus Used 69

Action Plan. 73
Action Plan Results 79
   Becky's Story 79
   Dawn's Story 84
Online Fellowship 91
Additional Resources. 93
Order Form. 95

Introduction

Psalm 103

*Bless the LORD, O my soul:
and all that is within me, bless his holy name.*

Bless the LORD, O my soul, and forget not all his benefits: who forgiveth all thine iniquities;

*who healeth all thy diseases;
who redeemeth thy life from destruction;*

*who crowneth thee with loving kindness
and tender mercies;*

*who satisfieth thy mouth with good things;
so that thy youth is renewed like the eagle's.*

*The LORD executeth righteousness and
judgment for all that are oppressed.*

*He made known his ways unto Moses,
his acts unto the children of Israel.*

*The LORD is merciful and gracious,
slow to anger, and plenteous in mercy.*

*He will not always chide:
neither will he keep his anger for ever.*

*He hath not dealt with us after our sins;
nor rewarded us according to our iniquities.*

*For as the heaven is high above the earth,
so great is his mercy toward them that fear him.*

As far as the east is from the west,
so far hath he removed our transgressions from us.

Like as a father pitieth his children,
so the LORD pitieth them that fear him.

For he knoweth our frame;
he remembereth that we are dust.

As for man, his days are as grass:
as a flower of the field, so he flourisheth.

For the wind passeth over it, and it is gone;
and the place thereof shall know it no more.

but the mercy of the LORD is from everlasting to
everlasting upon them that fear him,
and his righteousness unto children's children;
to such as keep his covenant,
and to those that remember his
commandments to do them.

The LORD hath prepared his throne in the heavens;
and his kingdom ruleth over all.

Bless the LORD, ye his angels, that excel in strength,
that do his commandments,
hearkening unto the voice of his word.

Bless ye the LORD, all ye his hosts; ye ministers of his,
that do his pleasure.

Bless the LORD, all his works in all places of his
dominion: bless the LORD, O my soul.

Psalm 103 is one of my favourite Psalms. It speaks about the many benefits of being a Christian and gives us a host of reasons why we should praise our Lord. He has redeemed us and forgiven us; healed us and showered his mercy upon us; he has crowned us with loving kindness and taken pity on us in our feeble frame. We have every reason for hope and praise and we need to frequently recall just how much our God has done for us.

Reminding ourselves of the benefits of faith in God is not something we are simply requested to do; rather we are to command our soul to "forget not all his benefits" (Psalm 103:2). Remembering how God has moved in our past will help to strengthen us for the future. It is good to think back, to learn from our experience of seeing our Father in action and to call to mind the great things he has done.

When I first became a Christian, God asked me to "Tell the world what you have seen me do." It was a simple calling yet one that I came to realise is so very important. How easy it is when we go through difficult times to forget or minimise the power of God. Tasks we face today seem impossible and yet yesterday God may have taken us over far bigger hurdles than we now face. Being reminded of what we have seen God do in the past is such a vital part of our armour for facing the future.

Initially when speaking to others I focused on the story of how I became a Christian. I had a dramatic testimony - moving from an anti-Christian background to an up-front ministry role. At first, this was a good story to tell but as time went on I started to hear myself say things like, "Two years ago..." or, "Three years ago..." or even, "Ten years ago..." I realised that I was relying on what God had done in the past in my life, rather than expecting Him to work today or in the future. My faith had become dull and my expectancy that God would act creatively around me had, if I was honest, dwindled almost to non-existence.

The stories outlined on the following pages are all true and in most cases can be verified by others. Where appropriate, actual names of those involved have been included and their permission for inclusion sought and granted.

Of course, each person mentioned in this book is a special, unique and wonderful part of God's creation but so, too, are you. We are all "fearfully and wonderfully made" (Psalm 139:14) and you will have your own stories of God's faithfulness to share with others.

The second section of this book aims to encourage you to remember those times when God has moved in your own life and to record them in such a way as to enable those memories to be of help to others. Sometimes we can gloss over our own experiences, preferring instead the more dramatic sounding stories of others. Yet God gives us what we need for the situations in which we find ourselves. If you have experience of seeing God work, albeit ever so gently, that is a testimony of His love for you. It might also, though, be for the benefit of others. Maybe it is solely for your own encouragement but maybe, too, there is a family member, friend, church contact or work colleague who would benefit by hearing you talk about your experience.

If we are serious about wanting to "preach the word... in season and out of season..." (2 Timothy 4:2) we need to work at sharing our stories, editing them down from a vague recollection to a sharp instrument that can be used to help, encourage and stimulate others in their journey of faith. This takes hard work, dedication and a willingness to share our faults and failings, as well as our strengths and successes. As you will see towards the end of this book, two people have agreed to share their experiences of "telling the world" and our united hope and prayer is that you will join with us in "forgetting not all (God's) benefits" and tell the world what you have seen Him do.

62 Piles of Grass

In August 2000 I married an American. We planned to hold the ceremony on the front lawn of his home in Baltimore, Maryland. Three days before the wedding, I flew from the UK with a long list of things that I needed to do before the big event and an equally long list for my future husband, Rick, to undertake.

The day before I flew over, Rick and his best man had decided to cut the grass so that the lawn would be in good condition for the wedding. Unfortunately, the lawn-mower that had come with the house had broken and the lawn had not been cut for weeks. It was about a foot high when they started. The only mower that was available simply left the cut grass lying on the ground. When they had cut the lawn, there was loose grass all over it. In short, it looked a mess. They decided that the only thing to do was to rake up all the grass and remove it bit by bit. By the time I arrived there were 62 piles of grass dotted over the acre of land, ready for collection. I was greeted at the airport by Rick, who told me that the next three days would be taken up with removing all the grass – ensuring that there certainly would be no time for anything else.

This was not good news! There were far too many other things to do for him to spend all day gardening! Having arrived late at night, I went almost immediately to bed hoping to catch up on some much needed sleep. Jet-lag however kicked in and at 4 a.m. I was wide-awake. Determined to try and get more sleep I stayed in bed. As I lay there in the dark, I heard the voice of the Lord speak to me. He told me to go outside to the piles of grass. Jet-lag can do funny things to the mind and I was absolutely convinced that this was not God speaking to me but a weird real-life dream based on discussions about grass the night before. I turned over and tried to get comfortable. There it was again – a clear voice that told me to go outside to the piles of grass.

Over the years I have learned to recognise the voice of God. Sometimes I get it confused with my own desires but this was certainly not something I desired! I looked out of the window. It was pitch black. I tried to reason with myself – surely God would want me to sleep. To be rested. Especially after an arduous flight and several busy months of activity. On the other hand, I have never been one to waste time and here I was, wide-awake at 4 a.m. doing nothing useful. Would it really hurt to get up, go outside and start to clear away the 62 piles of grass? I decided to get up and start work on the garden. After throwing on some clothes and grabbing the garden implements, I went outside to the front garden. The house was situated in a cul-de-sac – a no-through road with no passing traffic. Hardly a sole went past the house in the daytime let alone at night. I went to the first pile of grass and spent 20 minutes or so moving every blade into a bin liner, ready to move it to the compost heap later.

Then I moved to the second pile. As I did so, I heard a voice. I looked up and a lady was jogging along the front path. "Hallo!" she said, "What are you doing?"

Feeling rather foolish at being caught gardening in the dark in the early hours of the morning, I told her that I was moving the piles of grass. She stopped jogging and walked towards me.

"I know this might sound rather strange," she said, "but would you mind if I had all that grass? If you can't use it, my husband can."

"You are welcome to it if you want it" I replied. I couldn't quite believe that anyone could use so much grass and I had no idea what he would do with it. As far as I was concerned, however, it would be an answer to prayer to get rid of it all.

"If you could let me have your phone number, I will ask my husband to phone you later today and arrange to collect it."

I went indoors to find a paper and pen in order to write down the phone number. As I was leaving the house to go back to the lady, I again heard the voice of the Lord. He told me to take two copies of my book to her. My book, Capture Your Call, has nothing to do with grass whatsoever but I reasoned that God was probably right. One copy as a gift to the lady would be a good idea. I went to pick up one copy. I was just on my way out of the house with it when I heard God repeat, "Two copies." I went back to the bookshelf—obedient but somewhat frustrated at the obvious waste of giving two copies to the same person—and took them outside.

When I reached the lady, I saw that she had been joined by a friend. I gave each one a copy of the book, along with the promised phone number. "Oh how wonderful!" said the first lady. "I am a youth pastor at my church and really don't know if this is something I should be continuing with or giving up; I really need to find out my calling." The second lady, who apparently jogs every day with her friend but who had been held up on that particular morning and arrived late, was also in need of capturing her God-given call and despite months of trying had failed to find anyone in her church to help her.

The first lady promised to pass our phone number on to her husband and said that he would telephone around 11 a.m. that morning. I went inside, amazed at the apparent ease at which God had solved the problem of 62 piles of grass.

When Rick arrived for breakfast I relayed the story to him. He was sceptical. "You mean to tell me that at 4.30 a.m. in the dark you met a stranger who said she would take away all the grass and save me three days work?" he exclaimed. "Exactly!" I said. "Well I don't believe it and I am sure that her husband won't either. There is no way he will call."

Just then, the phone rang. It was the husband! He had called to speak to Rick to ask if he might be allowed to come and take the grass away. Rick was all too keen to grant permission but insisted that although he would like to be here to help, he had to leave the house around 1 p.m. when the grass would be collected and he would not be able to assist in the collection. "That is fine!" said the man. "I'm just grateful for the grass. Leave it for me to collect."

Even then, Rick was still sceptical. "I am sure when he sees how much there really is he won't take it all. And even if he does want it, there are bound to be lots of little blades left flying around the garden that I will have to collect before the wedding and that will take me the next day or two..." So it went on.

We went out to our appointment and about 2 p.m. that afternoon we drove back along the road towards the house. As we neared the top of the hill, we looked down and could see the house and the garden. The grass was perfect. Not one blade of grass was out of place. It looked as though a team of angel gardeners had arrived and swept it all by hand. Perfect.

Not only did this incident remind us of how quick God is to answer our prayers, wanting to help us in very practical ways when we most need help, but also of how faithful he is in the little things. Not one blade of grass was left. It had been cleared far more effectively than we could have done it even if we had spent several days on it. God sees the little things and cares about them. All we have to do is simply to invite him to take care of them.

"Be careful for nothing; but in every thing by prayer and supplication with thanksgiving let your requests be made known until God."
(Philippians 4:6)

The Art of Prayer

Is there anything that is too small to pray about? Sometimes the insignificant things can seem to us as though they are a waste of time for almighty, omnipresent God to be concerned about. This event convinced me that nothing is too small for prayer.

I have a spiritual director. A wonderful Franciscan brother gives of his time and experience to pray for me and to encourage me. We don't meet often but when we do it always seems like the most wonderful gift – something that spurs me on in my walk and service of the living God.

Shortly after one of my very first meetings with this brother, I decided to send him a card to thank him for his time. I went to the shop and looked at the vast array of cards on offer. Which one should I choose? Not being a Franciscan myself, and not really having much understanding at that time about the world of Franciscan brothers, I was keen not to send anything that might be offensive, upsetting or inappropriate.

I muttered a prayer under my breath, "Oh God, please help me to choose something special that will be a real encouragement."

Eventually I choose a small card with a piece of colourful artwork on it. Bright oranges and yellows, reds and ambers seemed somehow not to go with the brown world of the Franciscans but it was the card I settled on. I wrote a brief message and sent it off, not thinking any more about it.

A few months later when I next saw the brother, he greeted me with a beaming smile and grateful thanks for the card. It appears that he had received my card on the day he returned from a conference. Throughout that event, which took place at a venue many hundreds of miles from his friary, he had sat facing a large painting on the wall. As the conference rambled on, this brother had fixed his eyes on the painting and allowed God to speak to him through it. It had been a very special time for him.

Imagine his surprise therefore, to arrive home and open his post, only to find a card with exactly the same picture on the cover: something that he could place in his room as a constant reminder of the words that God had spoken to him.

Nothing, but nothing, is too small or insignificant for us to place before our God in prayer.

> **"Behold the fowls of the air; for they sow not, neither do they reap, nor gather into barns; yet your heavenly Father feedeth them. Are ye not much better than they?"**
>
> (Matthew 6:26)

Top of the Pops

It is not often that I wake up in the middle of the night but on this occasion that is exactly what I did. I awoke to hear shouts, screams and laughter coming from the street below. Reluctantly I got out of bed and went to the window to see what was happening. A group of about 8 or 9 teenage boys were walking down the road, attacking the cars that were parked on the street. Just as I got to the window, I saw 2 boys climb up onto the roof of my mini and jump up and down. Then they jumped off and ran to the next car at the end of the street to join their friends, before disappearing around the corner. A couple of the neighbours appeared on the road—clearly having been awoken in the same way—and I saw them call the police and take control of the situation. Figuring that there was not much more I could do to help, I went back to bed.

The next morning when I went outside, I saw that the roof of my car was far more of a mess than I had anticipated. The paint work was scratched and there were lots of indentations all over not just the roof but also the bonnet.

At this time, I worked for a Christian theatre company – a charity that had little money. We were given our board and food as remuneration for our work but hardly any cash. I could not afford to have my car repaired. This was also a very bad time to be without a car as we were in the middle of a run of performances that were taking place each day at a theatre on the other side of town. My car was needed to transport not just myself but a number of other people to and from the theatre on a very regular basis.

That evening my church home group was having its usual Tuesday night meeting at a nearby house. As I was performing that day, I could not attend but I realised that I had forgotten to send my apologies to the leader so on the way to the theatre, I called at the house to explain where I would be. The group leader came to the door.

After explaining that I would not be able to attend, I was asked if there were any particular prayer requests that they group could pray for me. I told her about the events of the night before and how difficult it would be to get my car fixed. She started to pray – right then and there on the doorstep. With just a few short, simple words, she asked God to somehow sort out the roof.

Just as she said "Amen" we heard a loud noise. It could best be described as a 'popping' sound. This was followed by a number of quieter "pops" – all of which were coming from the direction of the car. We went onto the road and looked at the roof of my car. There before our very eyes every single dent popped right back into place. When the popping had stopped, I got straight into the drivers seat and drove off. There was no evidence of anything at all having ever happened to my car – except, of course, a strengthening of faith both in myself and in my friend as we saw how quickly, how easily, how matter-of-factly God can hear and answer our very simple prayers.

God cares about loaves and fishes, money for taxes, our physical well-being. He is a practical God and He longs that we are practical in our prayers.

"And when Jesus knew it, he saith unto them, 'Why reason ye, because ye have no bread? Perceive ye not yet, neither understand? Have ye

your heart yet hardened? Having eyes, see ye not? And having ears, hear ye not? And do ye not remember? When I brake the five loaves among five thousand, how many baskets full of fragments took ye up?' They say unto him, 'Twelve.' "And when the seven among four thousand, how many baskets full of fragments took ye up?" And they said, 'Seven.' And he said unto them, 'How is it that ye do not understand?'"

(Mark 8:17-21)

House of Prayer

I have decided that the level of my faith can be registered at any one time by the kind of house I am living in! Each time I have bought or sold a home, God has been evident. The following three episodes show how God goes ahead of us to prepare each step of our path:

Moneyless Mortgage

On this particular day, I woke up with a start. God was whispering to me. Now let me make it absolutely clear at the beginning that this was not a normal occurrence. Yes, I was a Christian but I was certainly no more spiritual than the next person – possibly quite a bit less so! I had only been a Christian for a couple of years and I knew next to nothing about the Christian faith. I prayed and sometimes I saw answers to prayer but I knew at once that this was different. I woke up knowing that God was asking me to buy a house.

Whilst that might not be a startling revelation to some people, to me it was a crazy idea. Not only did I have no money at all in the bank but I had just given notice to my employer that I wanted to leave the company at the end of the year – just 3 months away. It had seemed right to resign and I certainly had a peace about doing that I but had no idea at all what I would be doing next.

I dismissed the idea immediately. There was no way I could buy a house even if I wanted to. However, the voice inside me grew ever louder, "I want you to buy a house."

For days I wondered around trying to reason with God that this idea really did not have any merit. Indeed, most of the time I figured that this probably was not God at all but my own selfish desires starting to come to the fore. Nevertheless the voice did not go away. Instead it grew louder. In frustration, I determined to prove to God that the idea really was a non-starter.

I made an appointment with the bank manager of a bank I had never been to previously. On the morning of the appointment I drew up a list of reasons as to why he really should not consider giving me a mortgage. After all, I had no money, no job lined up, no form of security and I had worked for the previous two years as an actress - not exactly a reliable profession.

I walked into the bank and presented my case. I remember the conversation started with me explaining why I was there, "I am here to rule out once and for all the possibility of getting a mortgage." The bank manager was intrigued. That was not usually the opening line of such an interview. He grew closer to listen. I presented my case and concluded with, "I know you can't give me a mortgage and that is fine but I need to convince my friend (that was God, of course, but I was too shy to admit that) that I really cannot buy a house."

To my shock, horror and surprise the bank manager laughed. "Miss Preston," he said, "you are a qualified teacher, a voice tutor, you have 2 years full-time acting experience and a background in PR. Most people who come to me have one skill and if they lose their job there is seldom any chance of them finding another. You are the kind of person who could work almost anywhere and you are the safest bet I have seen in a long time. You can have any mortgage you want!"

Within 8 weeks I had bought my first home – a home that was used by God to counsel, encourage and serve many people throughout the neighbourhood.

God's ways are not our ways. He can change circumstances in a flash. He is the holder of the purse and the keeper of the keys. What God plans and purposes, no man can thwart.

"For my thoughts are not your thoughts, neither are your ways my ways, saith the Lord. For as the heavens are higher than the earth, so are my ways higher than your ways, and my thoughts than your thoughts."
(Isaiah 55:8-9)

One Hour or Less

Three years after moving into the house described previously, I began to sense that God wanted me to move again.

I was happy where I was but I had by this time found a job that meant commuting to another town. The journey was elongated by having to cross my home town before reaching the motorway and travelling south to my new office. For 3 years I coped with the journey but God started to unsettle me and prepare me to move. Trying to be more sensitive to his calling that I had been when I first bought a house, I acted more quickly and placed the house up for sale.

The "For Sale" notice attracted visitors. Many people came and looked at the house, quite a few of whom even went so far as to put an offer on it. Days, weeks or months later, however, they changed their minds for no apparent reason and pulled out of the purchase. This happened many, many times. To start with, I was focused on God and trusted him to bring the right people at the right time. I shrugged off any change of heart by prospective purchasers and carried on with life as though nothing happened. After 6 months, however, the strain began to show. My hopes were raised and then dashed so many times that I got worn down.

One afternoon the telephone rang to tell me that the people who had put an offer on the property the week before, had changed their mind and would not be going ahead. I came off the phone and broke down in tears. I was frustrated and at the end of my tether. Out of sheer desperation I cried out to God: "I must have heard you wrong. I no longer believe you want me to move and I cannot cope with all of this. I am giving you one hour. One hour to sell this house and buy me another one or else I will assume that I got it wrong and you don't want me to move after all."

Immediately I had finished praying, there was a knock on the door. Although the "For Sale" notice clearly said that anyone interested in the property was to contact the estate agents, a couple had been passing and thought they would knock on the door and see if they could look around. Wearily and not of good cheer, I agreed to a quick viewing. Within 5 minutes they had seen the whole house and asked if I would accept a cash offer of the full asking price.

I was fairly shocked but deep down felt that they would do what everyone else had done which was to pull out in a week or two. To save argument, though, I agreed and they left.

I recalled my prayer. I had given God one hour to sell my house—and in theory at least that is what had happened—but I had also said that He had to find me another one within the hour. Wanting at least to do my part, I drove across town and went to the estate agent. I had visited many times before, trying to keep an eye on what was available. The manager recognised me and came to help. I asked if anything new had come onto the market since I had previously been in. She told me that there had been very little coming on the market but there was one property that was in the right area. I looked at the details. It was marked at £30,000 more than the very limit I knew I could afford. What was the point of viewing it?

Not having anything better to do, I agreed to go and look at it on condition that I could do so immediately. The agent phoned the owner who "just happened" to be leaving work early and would be there within 5 minutes. I drove over and met him at the property.

The house was great. Bigger than I had expected and well decorated. The one thing I had prayed for was a large garden and this house had one – even though it was covered in 6 feet high brambles and weeds! The owner asked me what I thought. "It is a wonderful house," I said. "Much better than I thought and just what I am looking for, but it is £30,000 more than I can afford. I am sorry to have wasted your time."

"If that is the only problem," he replied, "that is easily fixed. I will drop the price by £30,000 on condition you go ahead with the sale very quickly."

I went back out to the car and looked at the clock. It was 59 minutes after I had prayed. Four weeks later I had moved into the house, following a swift and uncomplicated sale of my first home.

God's timing is perfect. It may not feel like it sometimes but He does know what He is doing. So often He waits for us to be desperate enough to rely on Him and His strength alone. Then we see Him move faster than the speed of light – which after all He created!

"And God said, Let there be light; and there was light. And God saw the light, that it was good."

(Genesis 1:3-4a)

Choral Conifers

Five years later, I moved again, this time to a completely different part of England. For about 9 months I stayed in temporary accommodation whilst looking for the right house to buy. The cost of living in the south of the UK is always more expensive than living in the north and there was quite a gulf between the amount of money I could afford to spend and the kind of house I wanted to buy. Working from home necessitated extra room and this came at a very high price.

During this time, I met some other Christians. I shared with them my dilemma and they offered to pray for me and to help me find a suitable home. As one person prayed she opened her eyes and she saw by the fireplace a pine cone. She sensed God speak to her and tell her that the pine cone would be significant in finding the new home. This seemed a little strange to us but like Mary in the Gospels, we stored this in our heart and moved on.

For weeks I viewed one house after another. Each time we prayed and each time this same person mentioned pine cones. For one reason or another the houses I viewed did not work out and we continued to look elsewhere.

Some time later, a piece of paper dropped through my letter-box. The details of a house that had recently come onto the market were staring at me in glorious technicolour. This house seemed, for no apparent reason, to be much cheaper than any of the others and . I phoned and made an appointment to view. It was indeed a great house, in a good location and had the right price. I contemplated putting an offer on it. The words of my friend worried me though. Every previous time I had bought a house God had guided me clearly to the place where he wanted me to be. This time, all I really had, was a friend who kept seeing pine cones! I would be much more confident in going ahead if I had seen pine cones in my new house but search as I did, not one pine cone was evident.

Suddenly the telephone rang. It was the estate agent. He had just shown someone else around the house and they were likely to put an offer on it later that day. Was I interested in beating them to it with an offer of my own? Reason, common sense and logic told me to go ahead but where was God in this? I blurted out an offer and put the phone down.

The next day I had to travel out of town on business. As I drove back I chatted with the Lord about the house and asked him to show me what was really going on here. Was my friend wrong? Were pine cones a distraction sent to deter me from God's plan? Why were there no clear signs that this was the right house? Should I withdraw my offer?

In the midst of a traffic jam on the middle of a motorway, I heard God whisper to me, "What is the name of the house?" I had no idea. The documents all simply said it was number four. No name had been given to me. I couldn't recall seeing a name plate anywhere and I thought I must be hearing things – any thing but the voice of God. Nevertheless, there it was again: "What is the name of the house?" "There isn't one!" I shouted out. Silence. Then in the quiet, again came the now familiar words, "What is the name of the house?"

Instead of driving straight back to where I was staying, I took a detour and drove past the house I was thinking of buying. No name plate. As no-one was currently living at the house, I parked the car and wondered around the front garden looking for a name. The number four clearly beamed out at me but there was no name plate by the door. I started to go back to my car and then I saw it. Just above the garage, on a name plate that was so dirty, it was illegible, there was a name, "Conifers!" The trees from which pine cones come was actually the name of the house. I looked on the ground and suddenly saw a pile of pine cones to one side of the flower border. This was the house God wanted me to buy.

> *"And some of the Pharisees from among the multitude said unto him, 'Master, rebuke thy disciples.' And he answered and said unto them, 'I tell you that, if these should hold their peace, the stones (pine cones?) would immediately cry out.'"*

Luke 19:39-40

Does God Contradict Himself?

Around the World

The following story may at first glance appear to indicate that God contradicts himself; that he says different things at different times. It is the phrase "different times," however, that provides the explanation. It is important to realise that thefollowing two events happened over a decade apart.

When I first became a Christian, I attended a large church in the centre of London. As I was studying drama at college, it seemed natural to join the church drama group and to travel around the city, performing evangelistic sketches in a variety of services.

On one occasion we performed at another large city-centre church. A small team of us travelled to the building, spent a couple of hours rehearsing and then waited for the main service to begin.

Unbeknown to the others in the team, I had been pre-occupied with questions as to what I should do when my college course ended in a few weeks time. One possibility that strongly attracted me, was the idea of moving to Australia. The vast majority of my relatives and friends lived in Australia and I had always wondered about moving there. The quality of life seemed so much better and there seemed a large number of opportunities available there compared to the UK.

In the weeks leading up to this performance, I had been in regular contact with a number of people across Australia, many of whom encouraged me to move over there. As a Christian, though, I needed to be sure that this is what God wanted me to do. Although I was just a young Christian, I knew the dangers of doing things simply because I wanted to do them and I had no intention of doing that. I wanted to be in the centre of God's will for my life.

As we waited for the service to begin, I silently prayed and asked God to show me whether or not to move to the other side of the world.

The service started, we performed our sketches, we listened to the talk and we worshipped and prayed. At the very end there were a few minutes of silence for people to pray quietly before leaving.

Suddenly I was aware of someone standing directly in front of me. As I had been sitting in the middle of the drama team, inaccessible from the aisles, I assumed it was someone from the team wanting to speak to me. I looked up and saw a man I had never seen before. He simply looked me straight in the eye and said, "God does not want you to go to Australia." Then he disappeared. I glanced across to the rest of the drama team who were all staring in amazement and then glanced back in the direction the man had started to walk not 2 seconds before. I could not see him. He had disappeared. Literally disappeared. One of my colleagues simply asked, "What was that?" Not "Who was that?" but "What was that?"

To this day, I believe I saw an angel. A messenger sent from God to guide me in the right path.

13 Years Later

When I first became a Christian, God told me to "Tell the world what you've seen me do." That was my calling; to watch what God did and to tell others about it.

Right from the start that is what I have done. Every opportunity to speak I have taken and there have been many times when God did something in my life and then almost immediately afterwards he gave me an opportunity to tell others about it. Most of these opportunities, though, have been in England. Although I had travelled widely on holidays, I had seldom been given the opportunity to speak about God when overseas.

Following my experience in London mentioned previously, I did not go to live in Australia. I remained in the U.K. to live and work but my perspective on life remained global. I visited Australia on holiday once but quickly returned, conscious of the word of the Lord to remain in Britain.

At that time I had started to run training days. Small groups of people would come together for a day to study the Bible, pray together and to learn how to apply the word of God to their everyday lives. On this particular day we explored aspects of preaching and teaching; how to verbally share our experience of God with others in such a way as to maintain interest as we preached or spoke but also motivating our hearers to want to change their lives after the service.

At the end of the day I was very tired and longed to go home for a hot bath and early night to recoup some energy. However, just as I was leaving the training centre, I received a telephone call. A friend I had not seen for a while wanted to know if I would accompany her to a Christian meeting that evening as a visiting speaker would be there. I really did not want to go but as it says in Luke "a persistent friend gets what they want!" (my paraphrase) and a couple of hours later I found myself sitting in a large hall listening to someone speak about international ministry.

After he had spoken for an hour or so, he asked for people who had felt a call to international ministry to walk to the front in order to be prayed for. I knew that God had called me to ministry around the world but I was far too tired to go walking to the front. Despite the persistent nagging of my friend, I firmly resolved to stay where I was. I reasoned that God was just as much in the seating area as He was at the front and if there was anything He wanted to say to me, He could just as easily speak if I stayed in my seat! I closed my eyes to pray but felt such a lack of peace that I knew it was going to be impossible. I was aware that there was nothing "magic" about going to the front but on that occasion I felt a need to simply do as I was told and move.

As in many churches, those who arrive last are given the places at the front and to my horror I was forcibly pushed right to the very front of the queue and found myself directly face to face with the speaker. He put a hand on my shoulder and started to pray. As I closed my eyes I saw a very clear picture in my imagination of a globe. It was spinning. As I looked closely I saw an aeroplane hovering over the earth and going round and round the globe. The whole picture moved more and more quickly, gaining momentum as it went. I quietly asked God to show me what this meant and I sensed that He answered by saying: "For years I have told you that I wanted you to tell the world what you have seen me do. Now it will begin. I am about to take you to the other side of the world, to Australia. From there I will take you around the world again and again; so many times you will be unable to count them."

After the meeting, I told my friend what I believed God had said. She wisely suggested that we simply wait and see what happened.

The next day was Sunday, a day off and it was not until the Monday morning that I arrived back in my office. Immediately, I saw that a fax had been received. It was from a friend who lived and worked in Australia. He was faxing to ask if I would go over to Melbourne and work with him and his family for 6 weeks later in that year. The following year I spent almost 300 hours on aeroplanes and since then, despite a great deal of effort trying to remember, I have lost count of the overseas flights I have undertaken.

"The woman then left her water-pot and went her way into the city, and saith to the men, 'Come, see a man, which told me all things that ever I did: is not this the Christ?'"

(John 4:29)

It's a Dog's Life!

I wonder how you would answer if someone asked you if you would pray for their dog? In these days of wars, famines and earthquakes, drugs, violence and disaster, praying for dogs may not seem to be a high priority. Sometimes, though, God can use even a love of our pet to bring us closer to him.

In 2001 I received an e-mail from someone called Lisa. I did not know Lisa. We had not met before. Through the wonders of modern technology, she e-mailed to ask if it would be okay to pray for her dog. I receive a lot of requests for prayer and the vast majority are written down and placed into our prayer basket without too much care or attention. We do pray for each request but requests for dogs or cats tend usually to receive less time and attention than requests for physical healing or relationship restoration. On this occasion, however, I clearly heard the voice of the Lord. He asked me to reply to her carefully; to call her by name and to reinforce the gift He had given her of caring for the animals. I sent a simple reply. Back came a heartfelt appreciation that someone had at last taken her seriously. This led to ongoing e-mails, a decision for Christ and the nurturing of someone who has now become my right-hand person in on-line ministry. Lisa's story is remarkable. A testimony to the God who is the same today – in our modern, high-tech world, as He was 2000 and more years ago.

Here, in her own words, is Lisa's story:

Right There Where He Always Was

One of my favourite songs is by The Waterboys. It is called "The Glastonbury Song." One of the lines says "I just found God, right there where He always was." I always loved the song, it reminded me of a Christmas I spent with my father and sister. Now it means much more to me, because I have found God and He was indeed, "right there where He always was," just like the song said.

Let me tell you my story.

I'd often wondered about God. Where was He? Who was He? Could He and would He do anything for me? I used to live at a YWCA and a member of staff there became my friend. She used to pray for me when things were difficult. I found that very emotional and I was touched by her belief that God would sort things out for me. Sometimes I used to join her in prayer but I didn't really think that anything would happen. She assured me that it would. She said all I had to do was believe. But I didn't, not really, I wanted to but it felt like a risk.

I left the YWCA and moved to a new area. I have always had a difficult life. Things have been said and done to me that stunted me. I couldn't get on with my life because I was so badly affected by everything. I could hardly leave the house. I had no friends. I was bound by fear and memories. I was self-harming and switching from one eating disorder to the next as well as telling myself every day that I was fat, ugly, hateful and useless. I thought that with time I might get better but the years were passing and there was no improvement. I was scared of everything. Simply breathing and getting out of bed were an ordeal for me. I regularly contemplated suicide. I live with my boyfriend and whilst he was supportive in many ways, he was also partly responsible for some of my problems.

The only comfort I got was from the dogs that I sometimes looked after for people. I have a gift with animals, especially dogs. There is immediate trust and love between us and I was so happy that I could spread my gift with lots of dogs rather than just having one of my own. Dog-sitting seemed a great way to love lots of dogs. Then I got a computer. My journey began.

One lonely night a few months ago I was on a music download site and I noticed an advert in the corner that asked the question, "Can we pray for you?" I had a dog staying with me at that time called Max. Max is 16 years old and I adore him. He opened my heart to a love I didn't know. I wondered if it might be possible to pray for dogs? I decided to e-mail me and ask; after all, they could only reply and say, "No."

I clicked on the advert and filled in the prayer request box asking if it was possible to pray for my dog. I wanted him to be happy and comfortable and know he is loved. I submitted the request and wondered what would happen.

I decided that if someone replied saying that they were not interested in praying for dogs or animals that I would not have any part of their religion. Although I didn't fully believe in God, I did have an understanding that He had brought me and Max together and I couldn't understand why He would have done that if prayers about animals wouldn't be answered?

There was no need for me to have worried. The next day there was an e-mail waiting for me from Terry-Anne of The Framework Trust. It said that my prayer request had gone into the prayer basket and that they would pray for me. It said that God created everything and that if I had any other questions I should e-mail again. Well, I was full of questions! Who were these people? Where were they? What did they do? Could it be true that God had brought me and Max together? Had God given me a gift for caring for animals? They carried on answering my questions, there were e-mails going back and forth every day.

I felt a trust with Terry-Anne and all my questions were answered by her promptly and truthfully. She didn't pressure me or judge me. I told her that I was thinking about becoming a Christian but what did it really mean? What would I have to do? How would I have to live? Was it all about rules? Would I have to be really nice to everybody? Even people I didn't like? Would I be good enough for God or Christianity? Could God really help me? Wasn't I beyond help? Terry-Anne understood every single one of my fears and questions and one e-mail contained a simple prayer that I could say, if I wanted to, that would make me a Christian and welcome God into my life.

I read through the prayer and sat at my computer staring at it. All sorts of things were going through my mind. Was it really that simple? Could I really just sit here on my own and say a prayer out loud with no-one listening and all of a sudden God would be in my life offering me all the things Terry-Anne said He could give to me? I thought God was all about churches, not the internet? Would He really hear me? Was this what He wanted? People finding Him through e-mails and computers? But Terry-Anne had taken so much time answering my questions and she believed it all, she had faith in it so maybe it could happen.

It felt like I was daring myself to jump into a cold swimming pool. It felt like a huge risk and a gamble, I don't know why. Maybe it was about reaching out for help and putting my trust in some one and not knowing if I was going to be let down again. Was I going to be rejected? It can be so difficult to ask for help and sometimes you have to keep on asking even though it feels hopeless and it hasn't worked before. With all these things going through my mind, I took a deep breath and thought, "Just try it!" I prayed the prayer and felt like crying. This really was my last hope. I sat there wondering if I felt any different. Would I wake up the next day feeling happy? Would things start to get better for me? If God was going to help me work through all my problems, which one should I start with? It felt like I had a big tangle of problems and didn't know where each one started. How would I decide which was most important?

One big problem I had concerned the relationship between me and my boyfriend. There had been some terrible things in our past and, although he was very sorry for the things he had done, and had tried everything to make it up to me, I was very badly affected by them and couldn't seem to get over it. I didn't know if I should stay or go. I couldn't cope with my feelings of anger and resentment towards him, so how could we have a future?

I e-mailed Terry-Anne with these questions and she suggested I give the feelings that I couldn't cope with to God; simply to pray and say, "I can't cope with these feelings, so I am laying them at the foot of Christ and walking away from them." Again, I had my doubts. How could God just take these all-consuming feelings away? Could it be that easy?

I prayed as Terry-Anne had suggested and a few nights later a picture came into my head. I saw myself in a dark and dusty room. I was sat in one corner holding something in my lap and looking at it. When I looked closely I saw that it was all my hurts. I looked around and my boyfriend was in the opposite corner. He was looking at all his hurts. We didn't know that we were in the same room. I wanted us to look at each other, to see each other but we couldn't. We just sat there alone in our own private torment. The picture went away. The next day I thought about the picture and wondered what it was about. I decided that it was showing me that my boyfriend and I were too wrapped up in our own issues to notice and help each other. I saw that we needed to see each other and meet in the middle.

I decided to try it. I made myself available to him if he needed to talk and instead of thinking the things I usually thought such as, "How do you think I'm feeling?" I tried to put myself in his position. At the same time Terry-Anne was praying for healing for me, and for us, for peace and understanding in our relationship. My boyfriend must have noticed the difference in the way I treated him because he started to treat me differently as well. I decided to pray that I could forgive him. After all God had forgiven all of my sins so couldn't I find it in my heart to forgive him? It was gradual at first but then suddenly something slotted into place and I realised that all the bad things he had done were a long time ago. He hadn't really meant to do them. He had been to therapy to get help for his problems and he was plagued with guilt, so surely that meant something. I suddenly felt able to take another risk, I could forgive him and let it all go. The issue of our past reared its ugly head a few days later and I was able to look him in the eye and hold his hand and tell him from the very bottom of my heart that I forgave him. I told him that it was a long time ago and it needed to be placed firmly in the past; that we should focus on what we have now. We must remember the good things that have happened between us – like how we had cared for each other when we had both been seriously ill. How we had stood by each other in times of financial difficulty. The times when it seemed the world was against us and nothing would ever go right for us. The things we need to be grateful for.

It was like a release. Things started to fit together after that. It was a bit like building a wall. I had to get the bottom row of bricks stable before I could put more on top and I couldn't rush it. I had to take care with each brick and keep stepping back to look at it, making sure it was even and secure before going higher.

I'm still building the wall, even now, but it took that first brick to start it properly. If your home life is good and warm you can shut the door on the outside world and feel safe and loved. That helps you to cope better with everything else. Since then I have slowly started to feel differently about my life. I have started to take each thing from my past and have a good look at it and think to myself, "Right, that happened, I can't change it. I couldn't have controlled what other people did to me. It hurt. But now I have a choice. I could let it still hurt me or I could choose to put it in the past and walk away from it. It has made me part of who I am today and that is a good person; someone who can be compassionate to people who have experienced similar things. I can either let it keep on hurting me or I can use it for me and for others." Then I ask God to take it away – and the amazing thing is, He does!

I still have a lot of things to sort out. I will become strong and brave enough to let all of it go eventually but I have 27 years worth of pain to work through. Now, though, the world is starting to have colour and possibilities and when I have something difficult coming up, I pray to God to help me. I ask for an angel for the day to keep me company and stand by me. It has been like getting a brand new Father, the father I always wanted.

I am still in touch with Terry-Anne and will always be grateful to her because I really don't know what would have happened to me otherwise. We meet each week on-line to pray and to study the Bible. I have found friendship and trust – two very important things that I never thought I would have and didn't really believe in.

So, you've read my story and I hope it has inspired you. Maybe, though, you are thinking, "No, that couldn't happen for me. I've done some really bad things or I'm beyond help."

You are not, believe me, I felt like that but I was wrong. What have you got to lose? Just try it.

> 1. Ask yourself these 2 questions: Do you believe that God raised Jesus from the dead? Do you believe what the Bible says and that the only way to get eternal life with God is to trust in Jesus? If the answer is no, find a Bible and read Romans chapter ten, verses 9 and 10. Think about these words. If the answer to those two questions is yes – then move to the next step.

> 2. Say aloud, even if you are on your own, "God, your Bible says that if I put Jesus first in my life, if I make him Lord, and if I believe that you rose him from the dead then you will save me. I believe it! God, today I make Jesus Lord of my life. Forgive the things I have done wrong in the past. Help me to turn away from sin and to grow in understanding of you more and more. Amen."

You—like me—are now a Christian!
Welcome to the family!

*P.S. We still meet on-line to pray and encourage each other. Do join us. Simply go to **www.FrameworkTrust.org** and find out more. We would love to see you there.*

Wiped Out

The morning had started with lots of sunshine and clear views. It was a perfect day to set out on a long journey. My own car was in the garage being serviced and a friend had kindly allowed me to borrow his car so that I could attend a family celebration. It was a much bigger car than I had been used to and good weather was particularly important as it meant there was one less thing to be concerned about.

The journey there was uneventful but when I set out to make the return journey home, the clouds had started to gather. I had only driven about 20 miles of a 150 mile journey when the rain started. At first it was nothing more than fine drizzle but it quickly became one of the heaviest downpours I had experienced.

I searched around and eventually found the windscreen wipers. Within seconds of switching them on, the wiper covering the drivers side of the screen suddenly flew off the car altogether and appeared to land in a pile of bushes at the side of the road. Immediately the rain gathered on the windscreen and it became impossible to see where I was going.

I pulled the car over at the earliest opportunity and considered returning to look for the wiper. With long rows of bushes stretching back over the previous mile or so, and in windy, rainy and cold conditions I knew that it would be a fruitless task to get out of the car and search for the missing piece. It was far more likely that I would be run over by another car or would catch pneumonia than I would be to find the windscreen wiper. Nothing else for it – I had to pray.

Time was already pressing and I needed to get home that evening to ensure that my friend had his car for work the next day. Not only that but I too had to work the following day and was keen to get home as soon as possible; but how? No sooner had I wiped the windscreen by hand than the rain blocked the view again. I prayed.

I recalled the verses in 1 Kings 18 that described how Elijah had the opposite problem. He needed rain. He climbed to the top of Mount Carmel and prayed. He then sent his servant to go and look toward the sea. Seven times Elijah sent his servant to look out to sea and six times he returned and reported that there was nothing there. On the seventh occasion, however, he returned to say, "There ariseth a little cloud out of the sea, like a man's hand..." Almost immediately heavy rain started to fall. If God could bring rain like that to Elijah when he needed it, could not the same God stop the rain when I needed it? I prayed and asked God to ensure that no rain fell on the windscreen of the car for the duration of my journey so that I could arrive back on time with the car—and myself—in one piece.

The book of James tells us that when we pray, we should "believe and not doubt for he who doubts is like a wave of the sea tossed about by the wind. Such a man should not expect anything from God." To be honest I did not have much faith. I saw the rain all around and as I sat there in the car I could not see out of the windscreen at all.

I did, however, feel a compulsion to start driving anyway. Now if there are young children reading this I should stress that it is not wise to drive when you can not see out of the window! It is not something I recommend and it is not something that I would normally do but on this one and only occasion I sensed that acting in faith was important. I started up the car, indicated and pulled out on to the road.

I could see where I was going! Around the edges of the windscreen there were small droplets of water but the whole of the middle of the screen was completely clear and dry. I could see! The windscreen stayed clear for the duration of the journey and I arrived home safe, dry and in one piece!

> *"'Hear me, O Lord, hear me, that this people may know that thou art the Lord God, and that thou hast turned their heart back again.' Then the fire of the Lord fell, and consumed the burnt sacrifice, and the wood, and the stones, and the dust, and licked up the water that was in the trench. And when all the people saw it, they fell on their faces: and they said, 'The Lord, he is the God – the Lord, he is the God.'"*
>
> (I Kings 18:37-39)

Plane Prayers

Whenever I attend a Christian conference, I sit in expectation of the inevitable "plane story." By that, I mean that the person speaking will almost always include a story showing how God did something quite dramatic during an aeroplane journey. At one stage this became a source of great annoyance to myself and my friends as none of us ever seemed to experience anything like this – maybe because we hardly ever flew anywhere!

A few years later, however, after I had personally undertaken a number of flights, I realised that travelling on aeroplanes creates an environment that encourages us to be bold in speaking about Jesus with others. We are locked into a small space with a number of complete strangers – people we are unlikely to see ever again. The tedium of the journey and the fact that we have nothing in common with those around us except our desire to get to a particular place at a particular time, leads us to the point of desperation in trying to find something to talk about; and many people find flying a terrifying prospect – their fear being a natural way in for us to speak about our faith.

On one occasion I flew from Adelaide to Melbourne with two colleagues. We arrived at the airport in Adelaide about 3 hours before our plane was due to leave and the prospect of a wasted afternoon in an airport did not appeal to us. We went to the check-in desk to ask if there was an earlier flight we could be transferred to.

The check-in girl was extremely helpful and confirmed that there was a flight leaving about 20 minutes later. There were three spare seats but these were behind each other rather than side by side. We confirmed that we would be happy to sit in these and she amended the computer screen to show that we were to be allocated these seats. She then asked for our original tickets to be handed over and immediately registered that there was a problem. As we had flown at the cheapest possible cost, our original tickets had been sold to us with an agreement that these could not be changed in any way. It would not be possible for us to go on an earlier flight.

When she told us this, Kim and I looked at each other and started praying. We both sensed that God wanted us to go on the first plane but it seemed impossible. The supervisor was called and she confirmed that it would not be possible to change flights and we should be prepared to wait for the three hours. Kim and I continued to pray as they tried to change the computer screen back to how it was before. For reasons that neither of the staff could understand, the computer appeared to have locked and they could not take our names off the flight plan. In the end, the supervisor decided that it would be easier to change our tickets and to keep the computer as it was – so we were suddenly given tickets to the earlier flight.

We were extremely pleased to be able to get home sooner rather than later and we rushed to the departure gate only to see that most people had already boarded. We walked straight on to the plane and went to find our seats. Kim and our colleague were able to go straight into their seats but I had to ask a man to move in order for me to reach my own seat. He kindly got up and moved to the aisle but as he did so, he accidentally dislodged the armrest. It straddled across his seat, barring anyone from sitting down. He tried to move it back but it was stuck. A stewardess came along to help but it refused to return to its original position. A steward then joined them and between the three of them they managed eventually to force the arm-rest almost back into the correct position but not quite. The front bent slightly into one seat, whilst the back of it bent into the neighbouring seat. By this time, the man who was due to sit in the window seat had also joined us and he suggested that I take the more comfortable window seat, allowing himself and the other man to find a way of balancing the arm-rest between them for the duration of the flight. I duly obliged.

Because of the unusual start to our journey we started to chat. The man next to me introduced himself and told me he was on his way to visit his daughter who was at university in Melbourne. Between the seats in front of me, I could see that Kim was turning around and smiling. He had a look that clearly said to me, "I think God might do something here!" I turned around and behind me, our colleague had a very similar look. We had been speaking with others that morning about the power of prayer, especially the prayer of other Christians who are physically near by. The Garden of Gethsemane was an occasion when Jesus took some of his own disciples with him to pray, leaving them just a few yards behind. It was important to him that they were there and somehow on this flight it seemed important to me to be surrounded by praying people.

Shortly after we had taken off, I sensed that God was speaking to me. He wanted me to ask this man about his father. Surely I was wrong? I dismissed the thought but it soon returned.

Conscious of the fact that Kim was clearly listening to my every word and bound to hear me make a huge mistake, I turned to the man and asked him to tell me about his father. There was a strong reaction! "My father? Don't talk to me about my father. My father is a Methodist minister and I have no time for Christians or for God!" He went on to explain that as a child he had grown up conscious of the fact that his father seemed to be available for everyone in his church but never there when his own son needed him. This feeling of abandonment had grown even stronger over the years and he had never been able to forgive his father.

In the very next breath, the man turned to me and asked what I—a Brit or Pom—was doing in his country. After his outburst I was not relishing the thought of telling him that I was there at the invitation of the Anglican Diocese of Melbourne to work in local churches!

He started to apologise for his outburst and we talked further. He acknowledged that he did deep down believe in God but that his lack of forgiveness towards his father was causing him great pain.

At the end of the flight, we said our goodbyes and we walked off towards the exit doors. I remember seeing the man disappearing down the corridor and wondered why he was heading for another departure gate when he had clearly told me that Melbourne was his last stop. It was only when we were outside and waiting for a bus that he came running up and saying that he now had such a lot to think about that he hadn't noticed he was going in the wrong direction!

Chance encounters, or God-incidences as I prefer to call them – can be life-changing; for both people involved. Do not miss the opportunity to speak out whenever God imparts a seed.

"Some seed...fell into good ground, and brought forth fruit, some an hundredfold, some sityfold, some thirtyfold. Who hath ears to hear, let him hear."

(Matthew 13:8-9)

How to ✝ell the world!

How to Tell the World

If you have been a Christian for more than a few minutes, you too, will have a story to tell. It is quite likely that you will have your own stories to tell . Nothing is wasted in God's economy. If you have ever seen God change your circumstances, teach you something from his word, bring resources to your doorstep or call someone close to you to accept Jesus, you have something that will not only bless you but which may also be something that you could share with others. Times when we fail to achieve something or when the end result was not as we expected, can be just as profitable to share, as our experiences of success. Sometimes our weaknesses show more clearly how strong and powerful God is, meaning that our failures can be even better examples on occasions!

Not every experience is intended for public proclamation, however, and in this section we will explore aspects of knowing how and when to share our stories. We will also develop our own personal action plan so that we can continue to grow in effectiveness as we talk about our experiences.

Whether you are a confident communicator or a shy storyteller, this section is for you; use it to the full to develop your ability to encourage and empower the world-wide body of believers.

Action Point:

When reading the next few pages it will be helpful to have in mind one personal story or occasion when you saw God act in your life. It may be the occasion when you became a Christian or it might be a more recent event; either way, be specific. This will help you to apply the theory of story-telling to the practical aspects of your life.

Why Tell Our Story?

How can our stories be of benefit to other people? If we are to avoid simply speaking for the sake of hearing our own voice we need to keep in mind, and indeed, sharpen up, our motivation for sharing our experiences with others.

First, we need to focus on the fact that experiences that reveal how God has worked, are about God far more than they are about us. Because these events involved us in some way, naturally we associate our feelings of the time with our re-telling of the occasion. This can come across in how we relay the story and often can cloud the real purpose. Somehow we need to remove our own perspective and to see what God did, highlighting His actions and purpose rather than our own, so that the glory goes to Him.

Secondly, the things that happen to us could one day happen to others. The ten commandments tell us to 'Honour our mother and father' and whilst this undoubtedly relates to our own earthly parents, there is also an implication that we are to honour and respect those who go ahead of us in the faith. Likewise, if we can share our own experiences, the next generation might be able to prevent making some of the same mistakes and move on a little faster than we were able to. It is our duty to share those things that God has revealed to us for the sake of the next generation of Christians.

Thirdly, as we observed in the introduction, we are commanded in the Bible to remember the good things that God has done for us. This will remind us of how faithful He is and help us to build faith for the next obstacles life throws at us. It helps us to get ready, be prepared and to be on guard against all things.

Finally, the New Testament reminds us that we are part of the 'body of Christ'. God designed us to fit into a fellowship of world-wide believers. The experiences, lessons and gifts of one person cannot but be relevant to others in that same body. God did not make us to be independent individuals with lives that lack impact on others. He gave us a Christian family to which we belong and with whom we have a duty and responsibility to be real and open.

For consideration:

Have you had an experience in which an aspect of the character of God was revealed? Do you think it could be an encouragement to others if you were to share your story?

Are All Stories to be Made Public?

The gospels show us that Jesus was, on many occasions, selective about with whom he shared certain experiences. When he reached the home of Jairus (Mark 5), the Bible clearly states that he put everyone out of the room where the body of Jairus' daughter lay, except the girl's parents and the three disciples who were with him. This was something that was just for them. When the girl got up, Jesus simply told her parents to feed her and we can only imagine how the crowds outside reacted when they heard and saw the dramatic recovery. This story impacted the whole area, yet it was directly witnessed by just a handful of people.

Similarly, there are many times when Jesus healed someone but immediately told the recipient not to tell anyone about what had happened (Matthew 9:27-31, for example). Sometimes these people did not do as they were told and the consequence was that Jesus had to move on to another area. If God makes it clear to you that a particular story or event was just for you, do not be tempted to share it with others. Ecclesiastes tells us that there is a time for everything and today may not be the right time to share your memories.

We need to be especially careful when our stories implicate other people. It might be highly amusing to share how our children made a funny remark or did something wrong when they were young but how will they feel as adolescent teenagers when they hear the same story being re-told? If we do talk about experiences that involve others, we need to be sure to obtain permission from them before we publicly speak out, even if we are only talking to a couple of people.

One of the most frequent complaints from the children of people in ministry is that their parents relayed aspects of their growing – up to their congregations. Undoubtedly some of these experiences were appropriate to share and may even have been shared with the express permission of the child concerned but just because someone agrees to one story being told, it does not mean to say that their life is to become an open book. Respect for others is vitally important and we need to build integrity by requesting permission at appropriate times.

There is, of course, the possibility that they will refuse to grant their permission. What do we do then? Quite possibly we must refrain from speaking about the occasion. If we do not respect their answer, why ask them the question in the first place? Most people, however, seem only too willing to grant permission to have their stories told and once this is obtained we may find that we have their prayerful support as well as their experience to help us.

For consideration:

When you tell your story, are other people mentioned in any way, either openly by name or more subtly in phrases such as "my friend," "my husband" or "my colleague?" Have you obtained their permission in order to share this experience? Could you do so?

Who Could Benefit from My Story?

By now, we not only have a story to tell but we also have a reason to tell it and the permission of those involved to broadcast it to others. The next question to address is to ask who will really benefit most from my story? We would not throw a single polystyrene float into the sea where hundreds of people were drowning and neither would we launch a life-boat into a private swimming pool to rescue a lost toy. We need to take appropriate measures at appropriate times in order to achieve the maximum result.

When God spoke to Jeremiah, He did more than simply tell him his calling. He gave him a calling TO a group of people.

"Then the word of the LORD came unto me, saying,
'Before I formed thee in the belly I knew thee; and before thou camest forth out of the womb I sanctified thee, and I ordained thee a prophet unto the nations.'"

(Jeremiah 1:4-5)

God ordained Jeremiah a prophet but He didn't leave him floundering around to try and work out where his focus should be; He told him that he was to be a prophet to the nations. In the same way, God showed Noah that he was to build an ark and to take on board his family along with the animals. God calls us to a particular group of people. Who is God calling you to speak to? Who would benefit most from your story?

Of course, just because we are primarily called to speak to one person, a family, a community, a church or a nation, God might surprise us with exceptions to our primary calling. A missionary with a heart for the people of Malta, for example, may be offered opportunities to speak at her home church in the United States when on furlough; or a Christian doctor working in city centre Birmingham with Muslim men still has a responsibility to speak with his family of the things God has shown him. We need to be focused but ready for any opportunity that God opens up for us.

When an occasion to speak opens up before us, how do we decide which of our experiences to share? In order to ensure that we are most effective, we need to understand the lessons that lay behind our stories. A story such as 62 Piles Of Grass that was described earlier in this book can be used to highlight a number of different things, such as:

- God cares about the practical details of our lives
- We need to be open to hearing God direct us at unexpected times
- When God does something it is done properly and to a high standard

Services, Bible studies or discussions based on these subjects would be particularly appropriate occasions at which to share our own experience. It might also be appropriate to share over a cup of coffee with a friend who is struggling to cope with the practicalities of life but we do need to be sensitive. It can be far from encouraging, to hear how God miraculously rescued you from a situation but apparently leaves your friend to cope alone! We need discernment. We need to pray and ask God to show us when and where to share our stories and then to pray again for the courage to do as He asks.

> ## *For consideration*
>
> What are the key learning points highlighted by your experience? Be specific. Who might benefit from hearing your story? Someone at church? In your family? A neighbour? Or work colleague?

Medium for Communicating the Story

This book is called "Tell the World" and we are focusing on opportunities to verbally communicate our stories but there are also other ways to communicate. Parish magazines, school newsletters and church news-sheets provide regular opportunities for us to share our stories with a broader audience. The internet has opened up the possibility of writing for web sites or sending electronic newsletters to hundreds of people around the world, simply at the push of a button. Even texting our stories is now an option for many.

Some people find that writing down a story helps to crystallise the facts in their own mind and it can seem less threatening to send out a piece of paper or an e-mail, rather than stand up in front of a crowd and speak.

The creative arts can also be used in a myriad of ways to share our experiences and many churches are now using dance, drama, puppetry, music and the visual arts as an expression of faith and a medium for communication.

For consideration

How do you prefer to communicate? Talking one to one with a friend? Embroidering great banners for the wall? Or writing for the local newsletter? As an exercise, consider trying to communicate your story in three very different ways.

Techniques Jesus Used

Jesus was a master storyteller! Throughout the Gospels we are shown time and time again how large numbers of people flocked to hear him speak. Have you ever wondered why that was? Yes, he had a story to tell and certainly his actions of healing and miracles attracted attention. However, it is unlikely that the crowds would have followed him for such long periods of time, growing tired and hungry as they did so, if he did not communicate in a very special way. After all, the church leaders were in the temples most days talking about God – the very same subject that Jesus spoke about. What can we learn from his example of communication?

First, Jesus communicated simply. He used few words and plain language. It was local parlance and directly relevant to the lives of the people who were listening. When we speak, do we do so concisely and in simple language or do we get drawn into the occasion and take longer than we need to?

Secondly, Jesus asked a lot of questions. When communicating with people he often used questions to put the focus back on the individual and to make them realise the futility of some of their arguments. Often, of course, he knew the answer to the question but he asked it anyway – to help people make up their own mind about something.

The stories Jesus told related to everyday experiences that his listeners knew about – sowing seed, fishing, eating. When we tell our stories are we aware of the cultural situation in which we find ourselves? Do our stories translate? I was personally caught out with this just a few months ago. I was in Mexico speaking to some extremely poor people and I heard myself about to talk about an experience I had had on an aeroplane. I suddenly realised that none of the people there would have ever been on an aeroplane; they would not know what it looked like from inside and possibly had never even seen one flying overhead.

It is not only country borders that dictate the need for cultural relevance – the language of teenagers today is very different to the language used by teenagers even five or ten years ago. Are we able to communicate effectively to different age groups?

A very important point to remember is that Jesus was fun! He told stories about shepherds! Not politically correct, maybe, but certainly a concept that would have brought a smile to his audience. Are we lively and fun to listen too? Or are we dull and boring? Be honest!

Next, Jesus helped people to apply what he talked about to their everyday lives. Sometimes he simply told a story and did not help the listeners to understand it—he left that up to God to do—but there was seldom little doubt that if Jesus spoke to you, you needed to go and do something. When we preach or speak, are we as keen to send people out to change their lives; or do we simply seek compliments on the gentle way we spoke that day?

Then we need to remember that Jesus trained the disciples to take over from him. He helped them to make sense of the situations in which they found themselves and he made sure that they had opportunities to practice their ministry whilst he was still with them. Who are we training up? As we share our stories, we can also encourage others to do the same, allowing them to learn from our mistakes.

Finally, of course, and maybe most importantly, Jesus not only spoke with his mouth but he lived a life of integrity that backed up what he said. He did not talk about something and then go out and do the opposite. What he said, he also lived.

> ### *For consideration:*
>
> Are you developing a lifestyle of storytelling or simply telling stories of life? When telling your story do you use simple words that a child could understand? Are you brief and to the point? Are key points relevant to people and easy to listen to? Do you ask questions and help people to apply your message? Do you encourage others to share their own stories? Does your lifestyle back up the fact that God has spoken to you?

Action Plan

As with any aspect of life or ministry, if we want to improve the way we do something we need to work at it. Sharing our stories is no different. It is possible simply to tell someone else about our experiences and for them to be blessed because of it. How much better, though, for us to be prepared on all occasions, at all times and in all places, to share something that is relevant, clear and helpful with those God brings to us?

Having read this far, and having completed the "For consideration" sections, you will now be ready to establish your very own action plan for further improvement. This need not be formal or demanding of time or energy but a consistent practising and preparing for opportunities as they arrive will ensure that God will be able to rely on us to speak when the right situation occurs.

The following is a simple action plan that can be adapted to fit your own needs. Each section is a guide only and intended to provide a stepping stone to the next point but it is possible to omit some steps or add in others as you find most helpful.

Action Plan

Goal:
Remember what God has done for you.

Action:
Select 3 stories to share

Points to Note:
Choose 3 very different stories, if possible.

Goal:
Remind yourself of the story.
Practice speaking aloud.

Action:
Speak each story out loud.

Points to Note:
If you are not used to speaking aloud, find a quiet place, close the door and whisper the stories aloud to yourself.

Goal:
Focus on the real message.
Pinpoint the things God showed you.

Action:
Identify the learning points in each story

Points to Note:
If this is difficult to do, record yourself saying the story and play it back. Note just 3 or 4 key words that sum up the story as this will highlight the real message.

Goal:
Even if you are more comfortable with speaking rather than writing, it can be easier to edit on paper than to do it verbally.

Action:
Write down each story.

Points to Note:
Don't worry about the spelling or grammar at this stage. Simply write in a free-flowing way as you recall what happened.

Goal:
List the names of others who might be mentioned when you share this story. Approach each one and ask their permission to be included in your story.

Action:
Obtain permission for referring to others.

Points to Note:
To cover yourself and others, it can be helpful to obtain permission in writing.

Goal:
Think about the kind of people who could benefit from hearing the story – how old are they? Where are they? How many of them?

Action:
Identify the situations into which your story could bring hope to others.

Points to Note:
This will not be a definitive list as God can open doors that you had not expected but it is good to have a vision for success into which you can start praying.

Goal:

List all the possibly ways by which you could communicate your story – e-mail, speaking, letter-writing, newsletter.

Action:

How would you prefer to communicate your story?

Points to Note:

If you are not sure how best to communicate – try each different media. Which was most comfortable for you to undertake?

Goal:

Practice speaking in front of a mirror so that you can monitor how you are telling the story as much as what you are telling.

Action:

Practice sharing your story

Points to Note:

Using a cassette recorder to monitor your speaking is embarrassing to start with but can be very helpful.

Goal:
Asking people to be honest in their feedback is very important. Try and find people who are good communicators with more experience than you currently have.

Action:
Invite feedback from others you respect.

Points to Note:
Anyone can say nice things about what you do and say; being honest is more important and a mark of a true friend.

Goal:
Prayer, and maybe fasting, does not have to be done immediately prior to an opportunity arising. We can prepare in prayer now in anticipation that God will open doors later on.

Action:
Pray for opportunities to share your story

Points to Note:
Ask others to pray with you and to pray for you as you seek to share your experiences with others.

Action Plan Results

What happens to our stories when we work through the action plan? Becky Taylor and Dawn Davidson have offered to share their own stories as examples of how the action plan works.

Becky's story was very long when she first told it. Many of the details are interesting but not directly relevant to some of those listening to the tale. Outlined below is the initial version, followed by a shorter much more focused edition.

Becky's Story

I was brought up by loving, church-going parents. My grandfather, whom I dearly loved, was a Methodist minister. However it was to be many years before I heard the gospel in a way that really affected me.

In my early years my parents attended church and I and my brother and two sisters went to Sunday School. However their attendance slackened off and one of my sisters challenged them as to why we had to go to Sunday School when they didn't go to church.

I had a friend who went to the local Anglican church and continued to go with her for a while but our lives took different routes when she went to boarding school and I didn't. I probably went with her parents on a couple more occasions and then, entering my teenage years, I drifted away from church and connections with Christianity.

At some time, however, a certainty that there was a God, and that he came to the help of those in need, had taken root in my heart, and for the next 15 years I was, what I call, an SOS Christian. I called on Him, he came to my aid, and like the nine healed lepers I rudely failed to acknowledge what He had done for me, ignoring His presence until the next time of emergency.

During the next 15 years I met and married my husband, we travelled the world together and then settled down to have a family. I think our eldest son was baptised because that was the done thing to do, although at the time I remember feeling a discomfort about what we were doing and a niggling feeling that there was more to this than just a religious ceremony.

We moved from the south of England to Norfolk and it was here that my next door neighbour invited me to go to church with her. The people were accepting of me and always interested to know how my husband was getting on with his car-restoring hobby. (Church was actually a pleasant change from taking cups of tea to a pair of feet poking out from under a car!)

Then one Sunday there was an announcement that Billy Graham was coming to Norwich and would be speaking at Carrow Road football ground. The name Billy Graham rang a loud bell in my head as I had often sung a John Denver song in which one verse stated, "when I'm gone they'll lay me down in Forest Lawn with piped in tapes of Billy Graham." I'd often sung the words without having a clue as to who Billy Graham was and now I had a chance to find out who he was and possibly what was supposed to be on the tapes.

The stadium was packed and we sang new and familiar songs before Billy Graham got up to speak. He talked about the love of God, about how all people have built up a wall between themselves and God by the foolish and wicked things they have done but that despite these things

God still wanted us to know His love and receive His forgiveness. As Billy Graham related the events of Good Friday and how Jesus had died in my place, taking my punishment for me, he stretched out his arms wide and for a few moments it was as if I was alone in the stadium and Billy Graham was telling me and me alone. For the first time in my life the gospel made sense, and for the first time in my life I realised that I was actually part of that scene.

Billy Graham made his usual call for people to come out of their seats, to come down to the front and pray a prayer of commitment. I couldn't do it. I was sitting next to the vicar! If I went forward everyone would think I was doing it because I was sitting next to the vicar. So I stayed in my seat and envied every person going forward.

That was it. I'd missed my chance. It was too late now. A week or two later as I sat alone in my parent's lounge idly watching TV a documentary about Billy Graham and the recent Mission England came on. At the end of it they interviewed Billy and once again he outlined the gospel message to the interviewer but then turned to face the camera and looking straight out of the screen at me, said, "And for those of you who are sitting at home watching this, it is not too late to pray this prayer." He led a short prayer of commitment and I knew that I had made a real decision in my heart to follow Jesus.

Over the twenty years that have followed I have know God's hand leading me, holding me, loving me, comforting me and disciplining me not least of all when our four month old daughter developed severe fitting in the middle of the night and four days later died in Great Ormond Street Hospital. If I had not had the comfort of God's love around me what would I do. Those were my thoughts as I looked out of the window some eight storeys up. If life was so fragile what would be the point of living. This grief hurt more than any physical pain I had ever experienced before. But God held me tight and a caring church family supported us with comfort and prayer. Words from the Bible encouraged and healed me through my time of grief until I could look on Natasha's short life as a privilege to have had. Nine months of closeness as she developed "in that secret place" and four months of love and laughter in a secure and happy home.

Another song became a picture of that week:

On Monday He gave me the gift of love – we went for a walk and Natasha was snuggled up close to me in a baby carrier;

Tuesday peace came from above – despite the feeling God gave us His peace;

Wednesday He told me to have more faith – by now at the hospital we needed to trust God as we watched over Natasha with all the tubes and monitors attached to her tiny body;

Thursday He gave me a little more grace – time to read the Bible and be strengthened for what was to come;

Friday He told me to watch and pray – she just couldn't hang on to life any more and late that night Natasha died;

Saturday He told me just what to say – phoning the relatives particularly my parents who were looking after our other two children, aged 3 and 6, and then later in the day explaining to them that their little sister wasn't coming home;

Sunday He gave me the power divine to let my little light shine – we went to church and despite all that had happened I sang out my praises from a heart that was so grateful to God for staying with me through all that gone on.

Through the pain of loss God nurtured me and taught me to trust him with all that I have knowing that he will never let me go.

Edited Version

I was brought up in a church going family environment but didn't hear the story of Easter in a way that made me a part of it until I was nearly 30.

Until then I was what I would call an SOS Christian calling on God in times of disaster and ignoring Him the rest of the time. Billy Graham made it quite clear that Jesus Christ, God's son had paid my debt for me when he died on the cross and that all I had to do was tell God how sorry I was for all that I had done wrong and He would be my friend for ever. Somehow, even though I knew what he was saying was true, I couldn't respond straight away probably because I was sitting next to our vicar and felt that people would think I had gone forward because of him.

A few days later however I was given the chance again as Billy Graham challenged his television audience. This time I responded and so did God. I knew I would never feel the same again.

God has been with me through some pretty tough times since. Not least of all when our four month old daughter died. As we held her He held us, He loved us, He strengthened us, He comforted us and then gently put us back on our feet, focussed us on all that He had given us and promised to stay with us always. God has never let me down.

Working through the action plan has not only made Becky's story shorter, it has helped her to identify the people and situations who might be helped from hearing her story. Although she is ready to speak of God's love to anyone who asks, she is particularly suited to speak to people who may already be attending church services but who are not entirely sure they are Christians; she understands how people feel when they don't go forward at large meetings; she identifies with those to whom God speaks in isolation via a television screen; and above all, she can clearly explain to those who are deep in the pit of grief, how God can reach in, touch and transform us when we are lost in bereavement or sorrow.

Dawn's Story

Dawn confessed that although she has been a Christian for many years, working through the action plan was the first time she has ever actually written down her story. As she did so, she not only discovered she could shorten the story quite substantially, she also found that she could tell the same story in at least five different ways. Here, first, is the long version of Dawn's story:

I'd always believed in God and had attended Sunday school. As a child I used to pray before I went to sleep and at primary school did RE lessons, which were all centred on the Bible, so I was familiar with the teachings of Jesus.

However, as I grew, the prayers at night devolved into the occasional "arrow prayer" in times of crisis and church attendance was limited to weddings and Christmas. Around the age of 14, I thought it would be a good idea to be able to say I'd read the Bible through, so I got out my King James Version and began with Genesis. Half way through Exodus I gave up.

I was married in church at the age of 21. My husband had a similar "religious" background – believed in God and had attended Sunday school. But neither of us were doing anything with our belief.

After about 12 years of (happy!) marriage, I decided to hand in my notice at work and take time out to re-train for a slight change of direction.

It was during this period at home that one day, for no apparent reason, the song "Lord of the Dance" came to my mind. It was not a song I could recall from my childhood, although I'd heard it on "Songs of Praise" and elsewhere a few times. I didn't know all the words and felt compelled to go out and buy a CD with the song on, so I could learn it.

Over a period of about two weeks, "Lord of the Dance" went round in my head over and over, but rather than being a source of irritation (like some advertising jingles can be), the more I heard it, the more I was filled with a tremendously uplifting sense of joy. Eventually, I was dancing round the house to the song and the words "And I'll lead you all wherever you may be, and I'll lead you all in the dance said he" seemed to resonate and connect inside me – swirling and sparkling with an indescribable joy and freedom.

All this had been happening while my husband, Tim, was out at work and I hadn't told him about my "Lord of the Dance." Alongside the experience of joy, an impossible-to-ignore urge was growing inside me to go to church. I wanted to go, but I wanted Tim to go with me – I felt this was going to be important to me and I wanted him to be part of it. But I was not convinced that he would be keen to come along to church. So I began to think of how I could make the idea appeal to him.

One of Tim's interests is modelling small scale military figurines and part of this hobby involves a certain amount of research into military history. We were coming up to Remembrance Sunday and I recalled how, as a child, I had been taken to church parades (my father was serving in the army at the time) on this day and the pageantry and colour associated with them. A local village church, such as ours, would not offer such ceremony but it would be sure to have some sort of commemorative service…

I decided I would ask Tim to go to church with me for the Remembrance Day service and point out to him that it would be sure to touch on some military history because of the occasion. It got towards the end of the week and I hadn't at that stage said anything to Tim at all about my desire to go to church. I was in the kitchen, cooking our meal when he came in the back door. Before I could speak, he said "It's Remembrance Day on Sunday, let's go to church."

It turned out that over the same two-week period as I had been singing "Lord of the Dance" Tim had been feeling stressed at work and had started singing pop songs to himself to help him relax. Eventually he recalled the hymns he used to sing at Sunday school and began to hum those familiar tunes. He then said the thought came to him that if he liked these songs so much, why not go to church and sing them? He recalled me telling him about the Remembrance Day church parades of my childhood and decided he'd suggest we go to church then, as it might have more appeal to me!

Amazed, I told Tim my side of the story and we went along to the Remembrance Day service at our local Church of England church, expecting a traditional hymn sandwich.

We were surprised to find a lively charismatic church and a loving and welcoming church family. We didn't realise this type of worship existed in this country and after an initial (but very brief) moment of caution, we soon realised (after some biblical teaching) that this was all very "kosher" and embraced this style of worship with great delight. We were taken through a course on the foundations of the Christian faith and a few months later we were confirmed and able to take communion.

We made a commitment to Christ about four weeks after our initial visit to church and haven't looked back since. Filled with the Spirit and armed with an NIV bible, I read through it in less than a year and I know I will continue to read and study it for the rest of my days. It is just amazing to be in relationship with Jesus – He is alive, He communicates and He is faithful. We were happy before meeting God but with the Lord in our lives it is like going from monochrome to glorious technicolour!

Edited Versions

1. God spoke to me through the song "Lord of the Dance," ("And I'll lead you all wherever you may be, And I'll lead you all in the dance said He") giving me an impossible-to-ignore urge to go to church. My husband and I started to attend and almost immediately took a basic course in Christianity, so that we could be confirmed and join in taking communion. We were told about the importance of praying a prayer of commitment – so we did this about four weeks later, although we both felt we had already made the commitment in our hearts. We were happy before we came to the Lord, but having Him in our lives has been like going from a monochrome existence to glorious technicolour!

2. I've always believed in God and had a Sunday school background. As a child I would say prayers before I went to sleep. But as I grew, this habit devolved into an occasional 'arrow prayer' in times of crisis. Church attendance became a weddings and Christmases affair. It wasn't until, at the age of 33, I had an encounter with the living God that made me realise there was more to it than just an acknowledgement in your head that He existed. It had to involve relationship. As a result, my husband and I joined the local church, committed our lives to Jesus, and haven't looked back!

3. I couldn't imagine how I would have coped with my mother's death without knowing the Lord. Yet His timing in calling me to Him, was perfect. I asked Him into my life about 6 months before my mother died – at the time I had no idea that her illness would be terminal. Yet through it all there was a bitter-sweetness as I struggled to cope with her loss but all the while experiencing an almost tangible sense of His presence. It was a huge comfort to me when, through the words of a hymn my mother spoke of, and also the words of a children's bedtime prayer, I realised that she had put her trust in Him. He hears and responds to even the faintest cry.

4. We tend to overlook the obvious – that God is supernatural and often works in ways that are far beyond our own expectations. This was certainly the case when He spoke to my husband and I about joining the church. We each had similar but independent experiences as God used music, song and Remembrance Day to line up our thoughts and desires about coming to church. Without any prior discussion, Tim suggested we go to our local church for the Remembrance Day service – unbeknown to him, I had been

planning to make the same suggestion. We went along and shortly afterwards made a commitment to Christ – that was the start of our new life together.

5. Following a desire given to us by God, Tim and I went along to our local Church of England church, expecting a traditional "hymn sandwich" type of service. We met, instead, with a lively charismatic service, complete with hand raising, choruses, and a church family who obviously cared for each other on a more than superficial level. We were delighted with the sincerity and reality we found and soon made a formal commitment to God and became actively involved in the life of the church. We were taken through a course on the foundations of the Christian faith which really opened the Bible up to us and set us off on our walk with the Lord. We are on a journey of discovery, excitement and great possibilities!

In each of the above versions, Dawn has had in mind a target listener; someone who could relate to one aspect of her story as a way in to finding God for themselves. She is no longer restricted by telling her story in one way and she is ready at all times and in all places to share her own experience for the benefit of the kingdom of God.

Are you, also, ready?

Online Fellowship

Be sure to join us for on-line fellowship!

The Framework Trust hosts online church, prayer and fellowship meetings at least once each week. We discuss the Bible, chat about all aspects of the Christian faith and pray for the things closest to our hearts. Many people have become Christians on-line, had amazing answers to prayer and developed friendships with people from many different countries.

If you, or someone you know, have questions about the Christian faith, if you want prayer for an aspect of your life or if you would welcome an opportunity to share your story of faith with others from around the world, please do join us on-line.

To be involved, visit our up-to-date web site at **www.FrameworkTrust.org** The time of the next on-line meeting is on our home page and you simply click on the words "Join Us Now." You will be asked to give a name (real or ficticious) and then you will automatically be able to join us for chat and prayer. If you have technical problems, let us know and we will try to help.

Do join us. We want to warmly welcome you to the Christian on-line community.

Additional Resources

Additional Resources

BOOKS

CAPTURE YOUR CALL
£5.99.
A highly practical book for both personal and group use. Discover the plan that God has for *your* life. Hear God call *you* to a specific purpose. Discover new things about familiar Bible characters. Suitable for group or personal study. **CAPTURE YOUR CALL** is available from all good book shops or direct from The Framework Trust.

YOUR CALL IS WAITING is the American edition of CAPTURE YOUR CALL. It is available at $14.99 per copy from all good book shops in the USA or directly from The Framework Trust.
If you would like to order directly from The Framework Trust USA, please send a cheque payable to The Framework Trust to P O Box 3318, Baytown, Texas 77522.

TEACHING CD'S

We have a range of teaching now available on CD all priced at £6.00.
Order via the booking form at the back of this brochure.
Current titles include –

- **Crowning Glory** – *the crowns and rewards God has for us*
- **Capture Your Call** – *7 tips to help you capture the call God has for you*
- **Practical Patterns for Productive People** – *key transforming patterns*
- **Healthy Self-Image Affirmations** – *what does the Bible say you have? (Affirmations recorded with American male or British female voices -- specify your preference when ordering)*

SOFTWARE

Christian Goal-Setting and Achieving by Richard Allen Golko. A complete life-management software package to help you plan and achieve goals for your life. Cost: £69 (US$99) -- visit **www.ChristianGoalSetting.com** for more information.

Order Form

To order additional resources please send a copy of this order form, along with full payment to:

The Framework Trust
PO Box 293
Newton Flotman, Norwich
NR15 1TW

Item	Quantity	Amount £ or $
Subtotal:		
Postage*:		
Total Amount Enclosed:		

Send this order to:

Name: _____

Address: _____

Address 2: _____

City: _____

County/State:_____Postal/Zip Code: _____

Country: _____

Please allow 28 days for delivery. Thank you!

* Postage: Free to all U.K. addresses; add $5.00 for 1 to 3 items and 50 cents for each additional item outside U.K.